BRUCE'S AUSSIE DICTIONARY

PUFFIN BOOKS

PUFFIN BOOKS

Published by the Penguin Book Group
Penguin Books Australia Ltd
250 Camberwell Road,
Camberwell, Victoria 3124, Australia

First published in Australia by Penguin Books Australia, 2003

Written by Ben Mellonie
Illustrated by Jose Quartieri, Steve Williams, and Kar Heng Goh
Cover and text design by Steve Williams

Printed and bound in Australia by McPherson's Printing Group, Maryborough, Victoria

10 9 8 7 6 5 4 3 2
ISBN 0 14 330089 X

BRUCE'S AUSSIE DICTIONARY

Written by
Ben Mellonie

PUFFIN BOOKS

G'day,

My name's Bruce. I'm a great white shark, and it's been 3 months since my last feedin' frenzy. That's right, I'm a vego! Givin' up fish was the best thing I ever did. Fish who used to be prey were suddenly mates, I feel healthier than ever before, and now I've written my first book, Bruce's Aussie Dictionary.

I've swum all around Oz from the Coral Sea down to the Tasman, and up past Perth and the Top End to research all the colourful words that Aussies use every day. This book is chockers with everything from ace to zonked—and mate ... it's grouse!

In conclusion, I'd like to thank my editor, Fin Amy; my personal trainer, Barrycuda Duncan; and my sponsor, Shark Scott. Remember, fish are friends, not food.

Cheers,

ace

This is one of many words that describe somethin' really good. There are heaps more 'cause we Aussies are an enthusiastic mob.

e.g., We had an ace time swimmin' in the shipwreck yesterday.

Adam's ale

Water. This is not the type of water that me shark mates and me live in, but the kind that humans drink. It's fresh—no salt!

e.g., I can't imagine drinkin' Adam's ale. It has no flavour.

aerial ping-pong

This is another name for Australian Rules football. The game is most popular in Victoria and involves a lot of jumpin' and punchin' of the ball. This term is used sarcastically by those who prefer other forms of footy, like Rugby League and soccer. Frankly, I prefer to leave the ball games to dolphins and seals!

e.g., Turn off that aerial ping-pong on the telly, will ya? The League's on.

after-darks

Sharks. I used to take offence to this use of rhymin' slang. The last fish that called me an after-dark got eaten pretty quickly, but I've since learnt to stay calm when a cheeky fish has a go at me.

e.g., There's no way seals would swim in this water—it's teemin' with after-darks.

7

aggro

Short for aggravated, this means angry. This is how I used to get durin' a feedin' frenzy.

e.g., Anchor got **aggro** when I bumped into him with me razor-sharp fin.

ankle-biter

A child. I'm pretty sure humans don't really bite each other's ankles, so I suppose this is referrin' to the size of kids—only bein' as tall as their parent's ankle. That's Aussie humour for you!

e.g., Sharks aren't allowed near the beach, 'cause that's where the **ankle-biters** like to swim.

ant's pants

This is what you'd say when somethin's the absolute best.

e.g., Chum thinks he's the **ant's pants** just 'cause he won the race.

apples

When somethin's apples, it means it's good. Being a shark, I've never tasted apples, but humans seem to like 'em.

e.g., It's all **apples** here in the ocean since we found a shipwreck to hide in.

8

arvo

Short for afternoon, this is an Aussie's favourite time of day. Actually, the mornin' used to be my favourite time of day 'cause it was the best time to chase sleepy fish. Of course, I don't do that sort of thing anymore ...

e.g., I'm goin' to spend the arvo explorin' the reef.

... as

Use this phrase with any adjective to put emphasis on how you feel. Some examples are busy as, hot as, hungry as, etc.

e.g., Mate, I was stuck behind this sea snail durin' rush hour. He was slow as!

'ave-a-go-ya-mug!

Aussies love sport— they'll watch any game or event! This is the catchcry of the Aussie spectator, usually used to cheer the team on.

e.g., 'Ave-a-go-ya-mug!' I yelled at the walrus as he caught the ball.

9

B

back of Bourke

Bourke is a remote town in Australia. The back of Bourke is an even more remote place. Some parts of the ocean are pretty remote too. It gets deep and dark—and don't the fish look strange!

e.g., You won't find any sharks at the back of Bourke. There's not enough food there!

barbie

Aussies love to eat their food outdoors, and havin' a barbecue is the most popular way to cook when outside. Since Aussies like to shorten words, they call it a barbie.

e.g., Many a shrimp has met its end on a barbie.

bewdy

This word can mean heaps of things.

It can be the sort of thing you say when you're excited.

e.g., Bewdy! Another shipwreck to explore.

You can also use the word when you're referrin' to somethin' good.

e.g., Me new boat's a real bewdy!

And it's a handy word to toss round when you're talkin' about havin' an advantage.

e.g., The bewdy of bein' a vego is that you make friends more easily.

big bikkies

Big bikkies is a really large amount of money.

e.g., Some humans will pay big bikkies for a boat or scuba gear.

billy

This is a tin that humans use to boil water on campfires. Boilin' water seems a bit silly to me. How can you swim in boilin' water?

e.g., The poor bloke couldn't have any more tea after he knocked his billy off the pier and into the ocean.

black stump

This is the last outpost of Aussie civilisation. Australia's a pretty big place, and much of it is just empty space in the middle of nowhere, beyond the black stump.

e.g., Marlin and Dory had to swim beyond the black stump to find Nemo.

blinder

A blinder is a name for somethin' really outstandin', like when someone performs really well in sport.

e.g., Squirt swam a blinder in the race today when he won by two fish-lengths.

bloke

This is an Aussie male. Humans use the word when referrin' to their mates. Sharks use it too, of course!

e.g., Anchor and Chum are me best mates. They're great blokes.

blower

The telephone.

e.g., When I was feelin' the urge to eat meat, I got on the **blower** to me sponsor to talk me down.

bludger

Someone who is lazy is a bludger. I'm certainly not a bludger. It's hard work findin' enough food for a vego shark like me!

e.g., Those whales are **bludgers**—can't even bother to wash the barnacles off themselves!

blue

This word usually means a fight or an argument.

e.g., I had a **blue** with me old mates 'cause they wouldn't change their meat-eatin' ways.

It can also be used as a nickname for someone with red hair. Hah! I might be a shark, but I love a bit of irony! Don't ever call me a dolphin, though ...

bluey

This is how Aussie humans refer to a blue heeler cattle dog. I used to have a dogfish called Bluey.

e.g., I once saw a **bluey** swim way out past some surfers just to bring back a flipper for his owner.

13

bobby-dazzler

No, this is not a 70's rock star. This is a name given to somethin' that looks fantastic.

e.g., That cluster of coral is a real bobby-dazzler!

Bob's yer uncle

I don't know anyone who has an Uncle Bob, but every sea-dweller I know says this when things are goin' well or accordin' to plan.

e.g., To get to Sydney Harbour from the Great Barrier Reef, just follow the East Australian Current, and Bob's yer uncle.

bonzer

If Aussies are really happy or excited about somethin', you might hear them call out 'bonzer!' This word can also be used to describe how great somethin' is.

e.g., After the storm, there were some bonzer waves at the surf beach.

boofhead

This can be a name you give to someone who has a big head, but usually it refers to someone who's a bit silly.

e.g., That Dory is a bit of a boofhead. She can't seem to remember anything!

boomerang

As we all know, boomerangs are traditional Aboriginal weapons that—if thrown properly—come back to the thrower. Because of this trait, Aussies use the word to describe somethin' on loan.

e.g., Now, Chum, this vegetarian cookbook is a boomerang. I need it back before me party next weekend.

bottler

This is a name you call somethin' that's really admirable.

e.g., That Marlin really cares about his son. He's a little bottler!

brekkie

Breakfast.

e.g., Hurry up and eat your brekkie or you'll be late for school.

Buckley's

I'm not sure who Buckley was, but he was obviously pretty unlucky. Buckley's is a situation where there is very little chance of success.

e.g., Marlin and Dory thought they had Buckley's of finding Nemo.

buggerlugs

What you call someone when you're jokin' around—like you're pretendin' to be annoyed.

e.g., We're supposed to swim with buggerlugs over here, but I reckon he'll get us lost.

burl

Another word for try.

e.g., I know it's hard to give up eatin' meat, but you've gotta give vegetarianism another burl.

bush

There are few words that are more Aussie than this one. The bush is any wilderness area, and it usually describes a place covered by forest. I've never been to the bush. Why would I leave the water?

e.g., Many animals in the bush live off trees and plants just like some fish in the ocean live off seaweed.

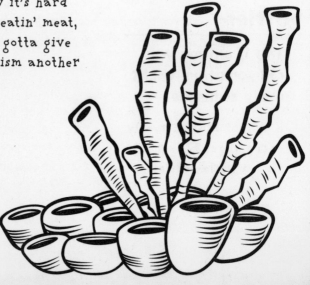

bush telegraph

Aussies don't mind a bit of gossip and the bush telegraph is a name for the word-of-mouth channel of gossip. The expression comes from a long time ago when many Aussies lived in the outback with only a telegraph to keep them in contact with the cities and the rest of the world.

e.g., Nigel heard on the bush telegraph that Marlin was lookin' for his son Nemo.

bush tucker

Tucker refers to food. Bush tucker describes the food you eat when travellin' through the bush. On dry land, this means anything from witchetty grubs and gum nuts to lizards. It's the sort of produce you won't find at your local supermarket.

eg., Marlin and Dory lived off bush tucker during their trip to Sydney Harbour.

C

cactus

When somethin's cactus, it's broken ... completely ... and can't be fixed.

e.g., Sorry mate, we can't take the boat out. The motor's cactus.

can of worms

This term describes a difficult situation that could be avoided if ignored. Some of me newly found fish friends LOVE earthworms, but I avoid 'em these days.

e.g., Don't ask Gill about his troubled past. You don't want to open up that can of worms.

carn

Aussies like to use as few syllables as possible when speakin', and they will often take long words and shrink 'em. Carn is short for 'come on'. You use it to urge someone on.

e.g., When I'm watchin' the footy, I'd often say 'Carn the Sharks!'

champ

This is a positive term you use for your mates.

e.g., G'day Anchor! How ya goin', champ?

chinwag

A chat.

e.g., Crush and Marlin had a chinwag while ridin' the EAC to Sydney Harbour.

chockers

When somethin' is chockers, it's completely full.

e.g., There's so much marine life in the Great Barrier Reef, it's chockers, mate!

choof off

Go away—and quickly.

e.g., You'd better choof off before that angry blue-ringed octopus swims back.

chunder

A playful word meanin' to vomit.

e.g., I've heard certain humans like eatin' shark for dinner. Even the mere thought of that makes me wanna chunder!

clanger

This is an embarrassin' remark that comes out of your mouth by a slip of the tongue. Clangers are often mean or insulting—but always accidental.

e.g., I dropped a real clanger when I called Chum a minnow.

Clayton's

This word describes somethin' that's a fake or a poor substitute.

e.g., Me vego friends tell me I have to try those soy fish burgers, but I reckon Clayton's fish would taste funny.

cluey

Someone who is cluey is really smart. I reckon I'm cluey. I've written this book after all!

e.g., Young Nemo is pretty cluey for his age. He thought of playin' dead so he wouldn't be given to Darla as a present.

codswallop

Aussie English is a really colourful language. This is my favourite word for anythin' that's not true.

e.g., The whale's stories about his days in the Northern Hemisphere are load of codswallop. His mates tell me he's never even migrated once!

corker

Anythin' that's really, really good gets called a corker.

e.g., Ridin' the EAC was a corker for Squirt.

cow cocky

An Aussie dairy farmer.

e.g., I once knew a cow cocky who gave up workin' a dairy farm to become a sailor.

crash-hot

Really excellent.

e.g., Dolphins think they're crash-hot just 'cause they can do flips and other tricks.

crook

Not feelin' well. Sick.

e.g., I had to cancel the vego meetin' last night 'cause I was feeling a bit crook.

21

crikey

When Aussies are alarmed or caught by surprise, they're likely to shout, 'Crikey!'

e.g., Crikey, that blue whale's huge!

cuppa

This word is short for 'cup of', as in tea or coffee, or, in my case, kelp soup.

e.g., Chum and I stopped for a cuppa before headin' to the Coral Sea.

curly one

A problem or challenge.

e.g., Marlin faced a curly one when he had to swim down into the darkness of the abyss.

D

daggy

A word to describe someone or somethin' that's out-dated. Aussies often shorten this word to dag.

e.g., Have ya seen that **daggy** submarine off Magnetic Island? It's a pile of junk!

damper

A type of bread made in the outback. It's usually round, doughy, and made over a campfire.

e.g., There's nothin' like a cuppa and a bit of **damper** to keep you goin' on a bushwalk.

dead horse

A long-term debt.

e.g., That dugong's been doin' night shifts to work off a **dead horse**.

It's also rhymin' slang for tomato sauce.

e.g., Those soy fish burgers taste a whole lot better with a dollop of **dead horse**.

dead-set

This word is used to emphasise what you mean.

e.g., I'm a **dead-set** genius!

It also means honest.

e.g., Are you **dead-set** about the size of that fish?

digger

This word was originally used to refer to an Aussie soldier, but now it's also used as another word for mate.

e.g., It's good to see you again, **digger**!

dinky-di

Somethin' that's genuine.

e.g., I'm a **dinky-di** great white, through and through.

24

dob on, dob in

Aussie kids would hear this one at school. It means to turn someone in to authorities.

e.g., Anchor dobbed on Chum to his vego sponsor after Chum ate a pod of seals.

dog's breakfast

A real mess.

e.g., Marlin told Nemo to clean up the anemone because it was like a dog's breakfast in there.

doona

A blanket filled with stuffin' that's used as a bedspread. It's known as a comforter or duvet in other parts of the world.

e.g., Darla pulled up her doona and went to sleep dreamin' of fish.

dooverlackie

A word you use in place of a name or term you can't remember ... or just don't know.

e.g., Sea urchins are covered in those spiky dooverlackies.

drongo

Anyone readin' this dictionary will be amazed at the number of Aussie words that mean slow-witted. Drongo is another one.

e.g., That young puffer's a good kid, but he's a bit of a drongo. He hasn't even learnt how to puff up yet!

drover's dog

This is someone or somethin' of little or no importance.

e.g., Some sharks get annoyed by the lampreys that swim round us all the time eatin' our scraps. I don't. They're like drover's dogs to me.

The word also means someone who works hard for little in return.

e.g., The life of a salmon is tough, all right. Those drover's dogs spend the last days of their lives swimmin' upstream to lay their eggs.

E

earbashing

Have you ever met someone who just wants to talk ... and talk ... and talk? What they've given you is an earbashing.

e.g., I got an earbashing from me mum when I didn't go to school.

easy on

This is a term Aussies use when they're tellin' someone to calm down. It's somethin' I say a lot at me vego meetin's when emotions run high.

e.g., Easy on, mate! We've missed the tide, but there'll be another one soon.

eat a horse and chase the rider

When I first became a vego, I had a hard time findin' enough food to satisfy me appetite. I could have eaten a horse. I was SO hungry, I could have chased the rider as well. Get the picture? Use this expression when you're absolutely starvin'.

e.g., I missed brekkie today. Now I'm so hungry I could eat a horse and chase the rider.

esky

These are boxes that humans use to keep food and drinks cold. They're pretty popular with fishermen and beach-goers. Eskies are usually made of plastic or foam.

e.g., I took a bite out of an esky that had fallen off a fishing boat. It tasted worse than a surfboard, but at least there were some tasty sandwiches inside!

F

face fungus

Aussies affectionately call beards and moustaches face fungus.

e.g., Catfish have whiskers that look a bit like human face fungus.

fair crack of the whip

This is used when someone is doin' somethin' that just isn't right or is sayin' somethin' that just isn't true.

e.g., Fair crack of the whip, Anchor! There's no way you'll get through that jellyfish forest without gettin' stung.

fair dinkum

This is a very popular bit of Aussie slang. It describes somethin' that's true.

e.g., That Nigel is a **fair dinkum** friend the way he saved Marlin and Dory from bein' eaten by the seagulls.

You can also use this word to question the accuracy of a statement.

e.g., Anchor is afraid of angelfish? Fair dinkum?

flat chat

This describes somethin' that's goin' really fast.

e.g., The manta rays swam **flat chat** to get away from the electric eels.

flat out

Really busy.

e.g., The Tank Gang were **flat out** gettin' their escape plan to work before Darla, the fish-killer, arrived.

flog

Aussies can be a confusin' lot 'cause many words can have a couple of meanings. Take **flog** for example.

It can mean to steal somethin'.

e.g., The oysters were in a panic 'cause someone had **flogged** their pearls.

It can also mean to sell somethin'.

e.g., The Stingray tried to **flog** me some pearls but I knew they were stolen.

footy

Short for football. There are heaps of games we call footy—rugby, soccer, and Australian Rules. But all forms of football involve kickin' a ball through goals at each end of a field.

e.g., Playin' **footy** with me mates is the best way to have fun and get fit at the same time.

full as a goog

A goog is an egg. This expression means well-fed.

e.g., After that second helpin' of seaweed, I was as full as a **goog**.

furphy

I like to tell the odd tall tale or two. Furphy is just that—a tall tale or wild rumour that's been told so many times, people believe it's true.

e.g., Did ya hear that **furphy** about the shark who gave up eatin' meat?

G

g'day

This Aussie greetin' needs no explanation, but in case you've been livin' on a different planet, it means hello.

e.g., G'day, Marlin! Good to see ya!

galah

Galah's are pink-and-grey cockatoos that live all over Australia. But there's another type of galah— someone who hasn't got much up top, if you know what I mean.

e.g., Divers who come down in cages are real galahs. I could smash right through those bars if I wanted to.

gander

A look around.

e.g., I had a gander at the giant clams, and, boy, are they huge!

garbo

The garbage man.

e.g., Wobbegongs are like garbos. They move slowly along the bottom of the ocean, eatin' everythin' in their path.

go troppo

Short for gone tropical. It means to become crazy.

e.g., Any fish is likely to go troppo after too much time in an aquarium.

good onya

Shortened way of saying 'good on you'. This is an exclamation of approval or awe. Sometimes, Aussies will shorten the expression even more to onya.

e.g., Good onya, Nemo, for showin' the grouper fish how to swim down and escape the net!

grommet

Grommets are young surfers.

e.g., Where's a turtle to lay her eggs with grommets crawlin' all over the beach?

grouse

Grouse is Aussie for cool—anything that's really excellent.

e.g., You gotta love the Great Barrier Reef. It's grouse!

grot

A grot is someone who's well overdue for a shower. You know ... a bit dirty ... a bit smelly. You can also describe someone or somethin' by saying grotty.

e.g., Bottom-feeders like a dirty patch of reef—the grottier the better!

grub

Aussies use this word in two different ways.

It can mean the same thing as grot.

e.g., Nemo, stop throwin' food and being a grub.

It also means food.

e.g., Let's stop at this harbour for some grub.

34

gum tree

This is what Aussies call Eucalyptus trees. There are many types of gums, and it's the tree most people associate with Australia.

e.g., The koala climbed to the top of the gum tree to get the juiciest leaves.

gurgler

A drain. Often used in the phrase, gone down the gurgler, which means somethin' has gone terribly wrong.

e.g., The Tank Gang's plan to escape went down the gurgler when the dentist installed the new filter.

H

hairy goat

Aussies love their sport, and horse racin' is on the top of many people's list. A hairy goat is a horse that never wins.

e.g., I love to goin' to the seahorse races, but I always end up backin' a hairy goat.

happy as Larry

If you're happy as Larry, you're very, very happy—probably 'cause you've had a stroke of good luck.

e.g., Ever since Marlin's been reunited with Nemo, he's been as happy as Larry.

hard word

To put the hard word on someone means you're givin' them a stern talkin' to.

e.g., I put the hard word on Chum. He had to admit he had an addiction to meat before we could help him.

heaps

This is another word for lots.

e.g., I love Port Phillip Bay. There are heaps of seals there.

hey

This short word can be used in a few different ways.

Said as a question, it has the same meaning as 'What?'

e.g., Hey? I didn't hear what you said.

You can also use it at the end of a sentence to make it into a question.

e.g., The current's strong here, hey?

And lastly, heaps of Aussies use it to get someone's attention.

e.g., Hey, Dory! I'm over here!

holy dooly

Yell out 'Holy Dooly' when you're amazed.

e.g., Holy Dooly!
Check out the size
of those waves!

hoon

A foolish, aggressive youngster.

e.g., That gang of sea
snakes is bad news.
They're nothing but
a bunch of hoons.

It's also someone who drives—or swims, in my case— really fast, and recklessly. You can use it as a verb, too.

e.g., The school of tuna
was hoonin' about in
the open water when
they swam right into
the side of a blue whale.

hoo-roo

Aussie for goodbye.

e.g., 'Hoo-roo!' said
the butterfly fish
as she gracefully
swam away.

iffy

**If you're a bit
suspicious about
somethin', you
might say that
it's iffy.**

e.g., I'm a bit **iffy**
as to whether these
algae clumps are
edible or not.

**You can also call
someone iffy if
you're not too
sure about them.**

e.g., I don't trust that
moray eel slinking
about. He's a bit
iffy if you ask me.

illywhacker

**Aussies don't use
this much any more,
which is a shame
'cause it's such
a bonzer word.
An illywhacker is
a type of con-man.**

e.g., That swordfish
is a real **illywhacker**.
He gave me a footy
that went flat after
the first game.

irrits

If you've got the irrits, someone has annoyed you.

e.g., Dolphins give Chum the **irrits**, especially when they laugh in his face.

J

jackeroo/ jilleroo

This word is used more often in the bush than in the city. It refers to a trainee on a sheep or cattle station, someone who's learnin' the ways of the land. A jackeroo is a male trainee, while a jilleroo is female.

e.g., The jackeroos woke early for their first day on the cattle station.

jack of ...

When you've become sick of somethin' or irritated with it, you say you've had jack of it.

e.g., Nemo had jack of Marlin thinking he was weak so he swam out to the boat to prove him wrong.

jiggered

Like the word cactus, this is a name you give to somethin' broken or worn out.

e.g., When the filter was jiggered, the water in the fish tank steadily began turning slimy and green.

jimjams

This is what Aussie kids call their pyjamas.

e.g., Put your jimjams on, Darla. It's time for bed.

Joe Bloggs

An average, everyday bloke. I don't consider myself to be Joe Bloggs. How many vego sharks do you know?

e.g., I wouldn't let just any Joe Bloggs join our vego meetin's. They'd have to prove they were serious, first.

jumbuck

If you know the words to Waltzing Matilda and wondered what a jumbuck is, here's the answer—it's a sheep.

e.g., If jumbucks ever went for a swim, it'd take ages for 'em to dry out with all that wool.

jumper

This is a piece of
clothing humans
wear to keep warm.
It's usually made
of wool from
a jumbuck. It's
called a sweater
or jersey in other
parts of the world.

e.g., Aussie kids have
to wear a jumper on
cold days to keep
warm.

K

keen as mustard

Keens is the name of a brand of mustard. If you happen to be feelin' really enthusiastic about somethin', people say you're as keen as mustard.

e.g., Nemo was as keen as mustard to go to school.

kick in

To contribute money for a gift, or help out for the benefit of another person.

e.g., We all kicked in to prepare a surprise party for Sheldon's birthday.

kick on

To keep on celebratin' or partyin', long after everyone else has called it a night. I was quite the partier in me day, goin' to one feedin' frenzy after another!

e.g., Chum and I used to kick on until four in the morning in our meat-eating days.

kindy

Most of me fish friends went to school when they were young, where they learned how to swim in a straight line, avoid predators, and catch food. Kindy is the first year of school for many young fish— and humans, too. It's short for kindergarten.

e.g., I met Chum on me first day of kindy, and we've been mates ever since.

klicks

Short for kilometres per hour, klicks are a unit for measurin' speed.

e.g., We're gonna have to go at 100 **klicks** if we want to make it home in time.

knackered

Knackered means tired, but not just sleepy. It's how you feel after swimmin' from Sydney Harbour to the Top End—and back again. Tired as!

e.g., Marlin and Dory were **knackered** after swimmin' through the jellyfish forest.

knock back

A refusal or rejection.

e.g., I **knocked back** the dolphin's invitation to play footy.

It can also mean to eat—usually very quickly.

e.g., I've never seen Anchor **knock back** so many sea cucumbers at once!

knock off

Here's a well-used term that describes finishin' work for the day. Aussies love this time of day, particularly when it's Friday!

e.g., I had to **knock off** early from a meetin' the other day to go to the dentist. One of me 3,000 teeth was sore!

46

L

lair

A lair is someone who likes to show off just a little too much. Every dolphin I've met has been a lair! They think they're so grouse.

e.g., Look at that anglerfish, flashin' his light. What a lair!

larrikin

A larrikin is someone who likes a bit of mischief, has a big personality, and doesn't mind havin' a bit of a stir ... a bit like me really!

e.g., Some fish think Crush, the sea turtle, is a big of a larrikin, acting the way he does at 150 years of age. I don't, I think he's ace!

laughin' gear

This is your mouth.

e.g., When I'm hungry, I like to wrap me laughin' gear around a big seaweed sandwich.

lie doggo

If your mum's wantin' you to do somethin'—like help with the dishes or clean your room—you might lie doggo. That means you'll hide somewhere to avoid having to help.

e.g., Sheldon lay doggo in his friend's place when his dad told him to clean his room.

little vegemite

Vegemite is a very popular spread that Aussies eat on toast for brekkie—it's a bit of an Australian institution 'cause no-one else seems to like the stuff. Young Aussies are affectionately called little vegemites.

e.g., Nemo's a top little vegemite—he's not afraid to give anything a go.

lob in

To arrive somewhere unannounced.

e.g., In me feedin' frenzy days, heaps of other sharks would lob in to fight over food.

lolly

This word has two different meanin's.

The first is to lose one's temper, as in do your lolly.

e.g., Chum did his lolly when I tried to eat Dory and Marlin.

Lolly also means candy.

e.g., Dr. Sherman tells his patients not to eat too many lollies so their teeth won't rot.

lolly water

This is what Aussies call sweet, fizzy drinks like lemonade and cola. I can't even begin to imagine what it'd be like to swim in that stuff!

e.g., When Darla tries to drink lolly water, the bubbles go up her nose and she makes a funny face.

lurks and perks

Lurks and perks refer to the advantages you might have in a job or situation.

e.g., There are all sorts of lurks and perks to bein' a shark. We're fast, we're fierce, and we rule the seas!

M

mad as a cut snake

This Aussie phrase means really angry or totally mad.

e.g., Anchor was as mad as a cut snake when he found out me and Chum went to the Drop-off without him.

mallee bull

The Mallee describes any of the semi-dry parts of eastern Australia that are remote and isolated. A mallee bull is a make-believe animal that's tough and strong enough to survive in such a place.

e.g., Not many sea creatures will mess with great white sharks. We're as tough as mallee bulls.

mate

Along with fair dinkum, mate is the most recognisable of Aussie words. It has a couple of meanings. Firstly, it means friend.

e.g., Chum and Anchor are the best mates a shark could have.

You can also use it to refer to anyone you are addressin', whether they are young, old, male, female, strangers, fish, humans, dogs.

e.g., I'd like to order another round of kelp burgers, mate!

min min

This is an Aboriginal term given to mysterious lights that are said to dart and float close to the ground in the outback. They're part of Aboriginal folklore, but even in modern times, sightings have been reported—luckily, none have been seen in the ocean.

e.g., The lights of a cruise liner on the horizon sometimes look like min min and they give me the creeps!

molly-dooker

This is a name Aussies give to someone who's left-handed—or left-finned.

e.g., I knew a shark who was a molly-dooker—he had so much trouble makin' a left-finned turn!

moosh

Moosh is the same as laughing gear—it's your mouth!

e.g., I got a surfboard caught in me moosh once and I couldn't talk properly for a week.

muckin' around

This is somethin' youngsters like to do—waste time and act foolishly. Some grown-ups have been known to muck around—or muck about—as well. Me? I'm too busy these days runnin' me vego meetin's to waste any time.

e.g., Stop muckin' around in the shallow water, Chum, you're scaring those poor surfers!

mud map

Mud maps are usually drawn in the dirt—or sometimes in the sand—to give someone directions when they're travellin' in remote areas.

e.g., Draw me a mud map to show me the way to the East Australian Current.

mug

Aussies LOVE this word and use it wherever they can. It means a number of things. Firstly, it's a word that can mean face.

e.g., Check out that stonefish. He'd crack a mirror with that mug!

It can be someone who is easily led or tricked.

e.g., You want me to buy your rusty old boat? Do you take me for a mug?

It also means to rob.

e.g., The barracuda followed Anchor into the shipwreck, intending to mug him.

And it's a word for someone fish don't like.

e.g., I reckon all fishermen are real mugs.

mulga

Mulga is an Aboriginal word that refers to the wood from a type of tree that grows in the bush. It's also another name for what Aussies call the bush—or any uninhabited place.

e.g., I wouldn't like me chances of survivin' in the mulga—there's practically no water there!

mystery bags

Mystery bags is one name Aussies give to sausages, which I've heard can taste pretty good, but some say are filled with ingredients that are best left on the abattoir floor ... yet another reason I became a vego!

e.g., Sea cucumbers look like mystery bags, but I don't think they'd go too well on a barbie.

N

nark

A nark can be a name for someone who's always complainin', or it can be the act of annoyin' someone.

e.g., Quit **narkin'** mate, there's nothing we can do about lookin' for your ball until the tide goes back out.

neddies

This is what Aussies call horses. Or seahorses, in Sheldon's case.

e.g., Sheldon's a fast little **neddie**—if he was in a race, I'd back him to win.

nellie Bly

Nellie Bly is rhymin' slang for eye ... or meat pie ... or fly ... in fact it can be used to refer to just about anythin' that rhymes with Bly.

e.g., Quit splashin' around, somethin's gone into me **Nellie Bly**.

never-never

This is about as far away from the ocean as you can get. The never-never is the desert that makes up most of Australia's vast landscape.

e.g., Just thinkin' about the terrain of the **never-never** makes a water-dweller like me shudder!

nick off

This is a playful way of sayin' go away.

e.g., Marlin really hurt Dory's feelin's when he told her to **nick off**.

no flies on

If there's no flies on someone it means they're cluey and sharp. Kinda the opposite of a drongo or a nong.

e.g., I'm the only shark to have ever written a book, so there's no flies on me.

no worries

Aussies love to say this when things are goin' well or they're tryin' to put someone at ease. Visitors from overseas love comin' to Australia because they think any country whose motto is 'no worries' must be a really laid-back, friendly place. They're right, of course!

e.g., No worries, mate—we'll get this shipwreck cleaned by the arvo.

noah's ark

I just had to include
this one 'cause it's
another rhymin'
slang for shark.
I sometimes wonder
if there were any
great whites like
me on Noah's ark.
I s'pose there must
have been 'cause
I'm here, aren't I?

e.g., The dolphins
stayed away from the
beach today because
there was a Noah's
ark swimmin' nearby.

noggin

This is a colourful
Aussie term for the
head.

e.g., You should see
Anchor's noggin after
he crashed into the
rock—it's got a huge
bump!

no-hoper

In Australia,
a no-hoper is
someone who
has no skills and is
doomed to failure.

e.g., I know a stingray
who's a real no-hoper—
he dropped out of school
to join a rock band
and he's tone deaf!

nong

This is yet another
colourful word for
someone who's a bit
slow. By and large,
Australians are an
intelligent, well-
educated mob ...
although they have
an awful lot of
words for people
who are otherwise!

e.g., That jellyfish is a
bit of a nong—his head
looks totally empty.

nuddy

Humans are the only creatures on earth who happen to wear clothes. When they're not wearin' them, they are nude, or in the nuddy.

e.g., Us ocean creatures are always in the **nuddy**— it's just so much better for swimmin'!

O

ocker

**Ocker is used to
describe or name
a person who has
all the personality
traits that Aussies
are known for—
a sense of humour,
a laid-back attitude,
and a vocabulary
that's displayed
in all its glory in
this book!**

e.g., I like to watch
footy, have a laugh,
and swim around with
me mates—I'm told I'm
a real ocker.

old cheese

**If Aussies use this
word around their
mums, they're likely
to get a clip across
the noggin 'cause
it's a cheeky phrase
used to refer
to their mums!**

e.g., Me old cheese
won't let me out
swimmin' today 'cause
I ate all her freshly
cooked plankton pies.

oldies

This is similar to old cheese but refers to both parents.

e.g., You should listen to your **oldies** 'cause they know what's best. Just look what happened to Nemo when he didn't.

old man

This is what an Aussie calls his or her dad.

e.g., I'm told I'm the spittin' image of my **old man**, but I've never met him. He must have been one handsome and charmin' noah's ark when he was my age!

once-over

This is to have a quick look at somethin' or someone.

e.g., The clown fish gave the anemone the **once-over** before decidin' to move in.

one out of the box

Somethin' or someone who's exceptionally good is often referred to as one out of the box.

e.g., That 150-year-old surfin' turtle, Crush, is **one out of the box**.

onkaparinga

This is rhymin' slang for finger.

e.g., The last time a diver tried to take my photo, I snapped at his onkaparingas.

oomph

When Aussies are referrin' to the amount of power in somethin'—like a car or a boat—they talk about how much oomph it has.

e.g., Those explodin' mines have loads of oomph—they knocked me, Chum and Anchor sideways when they went off.

open-air wrestling

This is a sarcastic name for rugby, which is a kind of footy. It's a bit more physical and brutal than aerial ping-pong, so it tends to be played by walruses and whales.

e.g., I've a spare ticket for that game of open-air wrestling tomorrow if you want to come.

open slather

Open slather describes a situation where rules aren't observed—like in a feedin' frenzy. The biggest, toughest shark wins any way he can.

e.g., At our first 'bring a fish friend' meetin', it was open slather—poor little fish didn't have a chance!

outback

I've already told you about the vast, dry areas of Australia like the mallee. The outback is the most popular name for this big part of the country.

e.g., Goin' beyond the reef is like travellin' into the outback—there's hardly anyone around.

outhouse

Most people have their toilet inside the house, but some properties still have a separate building outside where you'll find the toilet. This is called an outhouse.

e.g., It's a good thing the dentist didn't have an outhouse, or Nemo would never have found his way back to the ocean.

ow-ya-goin?

Aussies really don't like syllables! This is a quick and easy way of sayin' 'How are you doing'. This is the way to say hello to your mates.

e.g., Ow-ya-goin, mate? I'm as happy as Larry.

OZ

It's short for Australia, mate!

e.g., There's an amazin'
amount of fish life in
the oceans of Oz!

P

packin' it

This means bein' scared. Bein' a big, lumberin' great white shark, there aren't many things that scare me, except ...

e.g., The first time I saw a whale, I was packin' it.

paddock

A paddock is an area of land used for farmin', but in footy the word gets used as a name for the playin' field.

e.g., The whales and walruses played a tough game on the paddock today.

pasting

To cop a pasting is to receive an earful of criticism, or to receive some sort of heavy defeat, like in footy.

e.g., I copped a pasting from Chum when I tried to take a bite out of Marlin and Dory!

Pat Malone

Bein' on your Pat Malone means you're on your own. It's more rhymin' slang.

e.g., I've got a lot of mates in the ocean, but occasionally I like bein' on me Pat Malone.

pav

Pav is short for pavlova which is a uniquely Aussie type of dessert that has sweet crusty stuff on the outside and is filled with fruit and cream. Mmmm ... it's makin' me hungry just thinkin' about it!

e.g., Dr. Sherman has a weakness for the odd slice of pav, even though he knows it's bad for his teeth.

piffle

Piffle is what Aussies call anythin' that's silly or a load of nonsense—the kind of talk that amounts to nothin'.

e.g., Sometimes all that comes out of Sandy Plankton's mouth is a load of piffle.

pig's bum

This is what an Aussie says when he or she hears somethin' that's not true. It's really the opposite of fair dinkum.

e.g., You're telling me the whales are up for a win this Saturday? Pig's bum!

piker

Someone who won't participate. This person tends to opt out of things at the last minute after he or she has already agreed to get involved.

e.g., I'm not surprised that the barnacle's not coming to the reef party—he's such a piker.

pong

A really bad smell.

e.g., There's an awful **pong** comin' from those pipes near the shoreline.

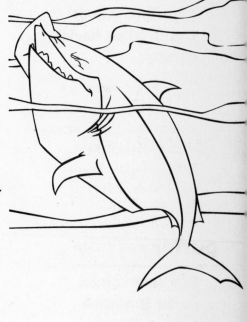

prang

Some Aussies love their cars—usually big powerful V8s and panel-vans. Sometimes they drive too fast and crash into things. This is called havin' a prang.

e.g., Once I swam up to the surface without lookin' and had a prang with a fishin' boat. Sure did give those fishermen a fright!

put the kybosh on

Puttin' the kybosh on somethin' means you've put a stop to it'.

e.g., My old cheese still thinks she can put the kybosh on me bein' a vego. I've got news for her ...

purler

Just like corker, purler is a name Aussies give to somethin' that's really grouse ... er ... good.

e.g., You should have a look at the eel's new cave—it's a real purler!

Q

QFRTB

These letters stand for Quite Full and Ready To Bust. It means you've eaten a lot of food and can't fit any more in.

e.g., After a feedin' frenzy, I would always feel **QFRTB** and it's one of the reasons I became a vego. I've gotta watch me waistline these days!

quack

This is what Aussies call the doctor. It's also used for one they don't really trust.

e.g., I went to see a **quack** about a pain in me left fin but he only looked at the right one.

Quick off the mark

As this phrase suggests, it refers to someone who is quick to respond to somethin' or act on somethin'.

e.g., When I was a meat-eater, I had to be quick off the mark to catch me food.

Quick-smart

This is how an Aussie describes the act of being quick off the mark.

e.g., You'd better get to the feedin' frenzy quick smart—all the fish are gettin' eaten.

Quids

This is a term used to refer to how strongly you feel about somethin'.

e.g., I wouldn't be a land-dweller for quids!

Quiet the worms

This funny little expression means to satisfy your hunger—in other words, to have a feed.

e.g., I'll have a little snack of seaweed in the arvo to quiet the worms before dinner.

R

Rafferty's rules

Whoever Rafferty was, he wasn't much of a rule-maker 'cause Rafferty's rules are the kind that don't exist.

e.g., There's no point whingin' about a feedin' frenzy not being fair, 'cause it's **Rafferty's rules** at one of those.

rapt

When Aussies are happy or excited about somethin' they are rapt.

e.g., I was so **rapt** when Dory came to another vego meeting. I thought she'd never speak to me again after I tried to eat her!

ratbag

This is one of my favourites and it's used in a couple of different ways.

A ratbag can be someone who's a bit mischievous—I've been called one many times.

e.g., Darla is a little ratbag the way she kills her pet fish.

It can also have a stronger meanin' about someone who's really bad—someone you wouldn't trust.

e.g., I wouldn't buy a submarine from an octopus 'cause they're such ratbags. They've always got at least one tentacle crossed behind their backs.

raw prawn

I'd have to say that most prawns I've met have been pretty good sorts, so where Aussies get this expression from, I don't know. To come the raw prawn with someone is to try to trick or deceive them. Not like prawns at all!

e.g., Don't come the raw prawn with me. I know where you were this arvo.

razoo

This is another Aussie word for money and it's usually applied when a person hasn't got any. For some reason, razoos are made of brass.

e.g., I'm sure most humans wonder how we sea-dwellers can live without a brass razoo to speak of. Much less hassle without it, I reckon.

ridgie-didge

Ridgie-didge is used by Aussies to describe somethin' that's true.

e.g., Marlin's story about his heroic search to get his son back is ridgie-didge.

right-o

Right-o is a bit like sayin' 'All right then' and it's what Aussies say when they agree to somethin'.

e.g., Right-o, let's get this cave tidied, then we can all get back to muckin' around in the shipwreck.

ring-in

This is someone or somethin' that's been substituted for the real thing. In horse racin', a ring-in is a horse that takes the place of another just before a race begins. It's a bit sneaky, 'cause it's not officially supposed to be there.

e.g., It was just my luck to back the ring-in. It didn't even make it past the finish line!

ripper

This is a word that describes somethin' that's really, really good, or is the name given to somethin' totally outstandin'.

e.g., Today's surf was a real **ripper**—the waves were the biggest I've seen in ages!

ripsnorter

This word's pretty much the same as the last one, but 'cause it's such a ripper of a word, I just had to include it!

e.g., Yesterday's swimmin' race was a **ripsnorter**. I beat Chum by a nose!

rugrat

Aussies give funny names to their kids and rugrat is one of 'em.

e.g., At Nemo's school, all the **rugrats** love to climb on Mr. Ray for a ride.

rust bucket

A rust bucket is a worn-out old vehicle that's well beyond repair.

e.g., Did ya see that old **rust-bucket** of a submarine? It's a wonder it doesn't leak!

S

Sauce

**Sauce is somethin'
I have heaps of—
cheekiness.**

e.g., I always pile on
the sauce when I'm
talkin' to sheilas.

Scrub

**To Aussies, scrub can
be another word for
the bush, or it can
be used to describe
the sort of rough
terrain you encounter
outside your normal
habitat.**

e.g., A squid once swam
across the channel and
disappeared into the
scrub. We didn't hear
from her for weeks!

Shanks pony

This is another old sayin' that applies to humans. Shanks pony is what Aussies call their feet and they use this to describe the feet bein' a form of transport.

e.g., It'd take ages to get from the Great Barrier Reef to Sydney by shanks pony.

Sheila

Sheila used to be a popular girl's name but somewhere along the line, some Aussie bloke decided to give this name to all sheilas ... er ... I mean girls—and it caught on!

e.g., I met some really nice sheilas at the party last night.

Aussie blokes will also occasionally use this word with their mates who might not be quite blokey enough.

e.g., Come on, Chum, don't be such a sheila. Swim with us to the Drop-off.

Skedaddle

As you know, I often got myself involved in feedin' frenzies. I'm not proud of it ... but I was what I was. Anyway, when a frenzy would start, a lot of the small fish would skedaddle. They'd swim away and scatter in a real hurry to avoid gettin' eaten.

e.g., You mackerel had better **skedaddle** or you'll get caught in those fishin' nets.

Squizz

This is another word for look.

e.g., I was late 'cause I was too busy havin' a **squizz** at the torpedo tunnel.

Skite

Skite means to brag.

e.g., I don't mean to skite, but I am a very BIG shark!

Skerrick

A skerrick is the smallest amount of somethin'.

e.g., I haven't got a **skerrick** of kelp left to give you—I ate it all up.

Steak and kidney

This is rhymin' slang for Sydney.

e.g., I love visitin' **Steak and kidney**—it has the most beautiful harbour in the world and it's great for doin' laps in.

Stinker

Stinker has two meanings.

In Australia—and in the ocean—it can get really hot, and days like this are called stinkers.

e.g., It's thirty-eight degrees in the water. It's a stinker!

On the other hand, a stinker can be a really bad person who annoys the heck out of you.

e.g., That seal is such a stinker—she keeps stealin' me secret stash of kelpcakes.

Stirrer

Someone who's always pokin' fun at others is called a stirrer.

e.g., In me younger days, I was a bit of a stirrer. I was always teasin' me mates, arguin' with me mum and generally makin' trouble.

Stone the crows

Bein' such an excitable bunch, Aussies have a number of expressions of amazement and stone the crows is yet another of these.

e.g., Stone the crows! Did you see the size of that whale shark?

78

stoush

Another sport that a lot of Aussies enjoy is boxin', and a boxin' match is often called a stoush. The word also gets used instead of fight.

e.g., Anchor and I had a bit of a stoush last night. I'd better go and make up 'cause he's a good mate, really.

strewth

Aussies sometimes get a bit emotional at times and strewth is one word a person is likely to say when he or she's feelin' frustrated or amazed by somethin'.

e.g., Strewth! I can't see a thing in this rough water!

strike-me-lucky

If somethin' good happens to an Aussie grandad—like backin' the winnin' horse at the races or seein' his team win at the footy—he's likely to shout 'strike-me-lucky!' You've probably never heard any of your mates say this, 'cause it doesn't get used as much these days.

e.g., Strike-me-lucky! The Dolphins won the aerial ping-pong grand final!

Stunned mullet

This is a way to describe someone who's been struck dumb by some sort of astonishin' event. Mullets are real dingbats and always have this really dumb look on their faces. I guess that's where this sayin' comes from.

e.g., Don't just float there like a **stunned mullet**—swim, or that speedboat's gonna hit ya!

Swifty

If someone tricks you into doin' somethin', you'd say they pulled a swifty on you.

e.g., That sea snake pulled a **swifty** on me when he convinced me to swap my favourite submarine for one that wouldn't sink!

thing-a-me-bob

Sometimes Aussies get a bit forgetful and can't remember the proper names for things. Instead, they give things a different name. Thing-a-me-bob is one of those.

e.g., Nemo was a little ripper when he jammed the stone into the **thing-a-me-bob** in the dentist's fish tank.

thongs

Bein' such a casual mob, Aussies like to wear casual footwear. The most popular casual footwear is the thong. It's a flat piece of rubber with a piece of Y-shaped strappin' that starts between the toes and secures the foot at each side.

e.g., If you wear **thongs** at the beach, you won't get stung by any nasty stonefish.

tippety-run

This is a special form of backyard cricket where the batsman has to run every time he hits the ball. In regular cricket, the batsman can choose if he runs or not.

e.g., Rugrats sometimes play tippety-run cricket at the beach. I don't know where they get the energy from for all that runnin' around!

toey

To get toey means to get nervous or anxious about somethin'.

e.g., I get toey every time I think about divers.

togs

Togs are what many Aussies call their swimwear. Aussies are big fans of the beach and will usually wear togs when they're there.

e.g., If I owned a pair of togs, I'd call 'em me Great Barrier Briefs!

toorak tractor

This is a vehicle being used in a location it wasn't designed for. 4-wheel-drive vehicles are designed to drive through the rough terrain and are popular with people who live in the bush. When people from the city own them, they mostly use them for pickin' up the ankle biters from school or doin' the shoppin', tasks that a normal car can do quite easily.

e.g., I reckon most of the toorak tractors that bring the ankle-biters to the beach have never been anywhere near the outback.

top End

The Top End refers to the northernmost part of Australia, usually the top part of Northern Territory. On a map, it literally is the top end of this wide land.

e.g., When you're swimmin' in the Top End, you've gotta watch out for me snappy mates, the saltwater crocodiles.

true-blue

This is another Aussie expression that is used to describe somethin' that's genuine or real.

e.g., The words in this dictionary are all true-blue Aussie words.

tucker

In a word ... food.

e.g., My favourite tucker at the moment is seaweed. It's nutritious, tastes good, and there's no shortage of it in my neck of the ocean.

two-up

This is more of an Aussie tradition than a slang word. Two-up is the name of a game that involves tossin' two coins in the air and placin' bets on which way up the coins will land. I've included it because it's a uniquely Aussie game and was as popular in the old days as footy and horse racin' are today.

e.g., When we played two-up with the octopus, it turned into a game of 16-up!

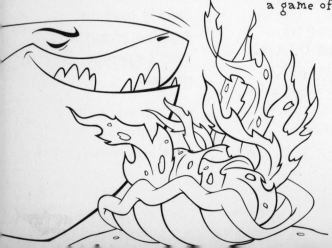

U

uey

Livin' in the ocean requires a lot of skilful swimmin', and this is one of the many skills I learnt as an ankle biter. Pronounced, 'you-ee,' this is the way the Aussies say U-turn, which is to swim in one direction, then turn around and swim back in the other direction without stoppin'.

e.g., I did a swift **uey** at the sight of the bottom of that fishin' boat.

ugg boot

Ugg boots are a type of winter footware, favoured by Aussie humans, made from sheepskin. I reckon ugg is short for ugly, but if I said that to some Aussies they'd have me for breakfast!

e.g., After seein' all his patients, Dr. Sherman likes to slip on a pair of **ugg boots** and relax in his chair for a while.

unco

When Aussies are a bit clumsy, they're said to be unco or uncoordinated.

e.g., I knew an octopus who was so unco, he couldn't tell his left arm from his right, from his left, from his right, from his left.

up the spout

If somethin's up the spout it means it's ruined.

e.g., The Tank Gang thought their escape plan went up the spout when Nemo's first attempt to jam the filter failed.

ute

Rhymes with cute. True-blue Aussie blokes love their utes. It's short for utility and it refers to a type of road vehicle that has a cab up front for the driver and a tray at the back to cart stuff.

e.g., I always avoid fishin' boats 'cause I don't want to end up in the back of a fisherman's ute with my tail hangin' over the end!

vee Dub

As with lots of other examples in this dictionary, Aussies love to shorten words to make them easier to say. A Vee Dub is a way of sayin' the letters VW, which, in turn, is short for Volkswagen, a type of car.

e.g., Somebody once told me that a **Vee Dub** will float if driven into the sea, but I don't reckon that theory holds water!

vego

Vegetarian is a pretty long word, so Aussies shorten it to vego. The 'g' is pronounced like a 'j'.

e.g., Bein' a **vego** has made me see fish as friends, not food.

walkabout

Walkabout was actually coined by the Aboriginal people of Australia—the original Aussies—who have a tradition of goin' for a long walk in the outback as a way to clear the head. We use it to mean wanderin' off or just not around.

e.g., Dory often finds herself on **walkabout** by accident, 'cause she can never remember why she's goin' somewhere.

wally

Dingbat, drongo, nong, etc. This is another name for those who are challenged by life itself ... you know ... a bit dumb. Wally is probably my favourite.

e.g., I felt like a real **wally** when I tried to eat Marlin and Dory.

waltzing Matilda

Waltzing Matilda is the name of Australia's most famous bush song about a swagman who wanders the land. To go waltzing Matilda is very much like goin' walkabout, but carryin' a swag—a bag of one's belongings tied to a stick and carried over the shoulder. Matilda is slang for a swag.

e.g., You won't find me goin' waltzing Matilda—I love livin' in the reef too much.

whacker

A whacker is someone who's a bit crazy ... nuts ... bonkers.

e.g., Dory's a bit of a whacker, the way she keeps forgettin' things.

whinge

When somethin's buggin' us Aussies, this is what we'll do. We'll have a whinge about it, that is, we'll complain.

e.g., I get a bit sick of hearin' me mum whinge about me becomin' a vego.

who-ha

A who-ha is any situation where someone creates a fuss.

e.g., Anchor made one heck of a who-ha when I told him I'd made friends with a dolphin.

whole box and dice

If Aussies are talkin' about the complete contents of somethin', they might refer to it as, the whole box and dice.

e.g., A cheeky shark swam into a fisherman's catch and ate the whole box and dice.

wigwam for a goose's bridle

Sometimes certain objects can't be identified, or Aussies don't want them identified. If an Aussie is asked what somethin' is, and he or she doesn't know, or doesn't want to say, that person might say it's a wigwam for a goose's bridle. It's a bit of a nonsense term so it just confuses the other person even more.

e.g., Anchor: 'I found this strange, round, metal thing on the ocean floor—do you know what it is?'

Chum: 'Looks like a wigwam for goose's bridle.'

Anchor: 'Didn't think you'd know, ya galah!'

willy-nilly

Anythin' that happens without thought or organization.

e.g., I used to swim into schools of fish and eat them willy-nilly.

witchetty grub

This is an example of bush tucker. A witchetty grub is a larval insect, like a caterpillar, and I'm told it tastes pretty good. Lucky for witchetty grubs, we don't find 'em in the ocean, 'cause if we did I'd have a hard time keepin' me jaws off 'em!

e.g., I once saw a witchetty grub on the end of a fisherman's hook. It didn't take long for a hungry barracuda to find it and gobble it up.

wobbly

When Aussies get all worked up and lose their temper, they're said to throw a wobbly.

e.g., I threw a wobbly when the diver stuck his camera in my face. He's lucky I didn't throw anythin' else at him!

wonky

If somethin's wonky it means it's a bit unstable—or not quite right.

e.g., I still feel a bit wonky after gettin' that smell of Dory's blood.

woop woop

Australia has a lot
of remote, out-of-
the-way places and
an Aussie will refer
to these places
as, woop woop,
especially if they
have to travel
a long way to
get there.

e.g., I had to swim all
the way to woop woop
just to see a manta
ray about a dogfish.

Wowser

A wowser is someone
who is just a bit too
proper and objects
to any sort of fun.

e.g., Don't invite
wowsers to reef
parties 'cause they'll
just dampen the mood.

Y

yabby

Small, freshwater crayfish. I hear they're feisty little creatures, with a mean pinch.

e.g., If a yabby ever met a crab, I'd say the **yabby** would make mincemeat of him.

yahoo

Yahoo is used to describe someone, usually a youngster, who's carryin' on and partyin' in a loud fashion.

e.g., Dolphins are a bunch of **yahoos**—you can't have a chat with any of 'em without 'em all laughin' and splashin' about.

yakka

Aussies don't mind a bit of hard work ... or yakka ... especially those who live in the bush.

e.g., Tryin' to catch crabs used to be hard yakka.

yapping

This is another word for talkin'.

e.g., Sometimes I can't hear myself think with all those yapping clams.

yonks

Aussies refer to a really long period of time as yonks.

e.g., It's been yonks since I've had a meal ... I'm starvin'!

youse

I remember me mum tryin' to get me to stop sayin' this 'cause it's considered a bit uncouth. Aussies like their language simple, and this one takes the cake. It's used as a way of addressin' a group. Instead of saying 'you people', Aussies will say 'youse'.

e.g., Hey, barracudas! If any of youse hassle me fish friends, I'll turn youse into bait!

Yowie

North America has Big Foot, Asia has the Yeti, and Australia has the Yowie. Some people believe this is a tall, ape-like creature livin' in the outback.

e.g., I'm not sure about the existence of **Yowies**. I reckon most of the photos that have been taken are just some galah in a gorilla suit jumpin' around like a whacker!

zonked

**This is the last word
in my dictionary,
and it's a great
Aussie term for bein'
completely drained
of energy after
a long day's work.**

e.g., I'm so zonked
from writin' this
dictionary, I need
a holiday to relax
and recover. I hear
the Bahamas are nice
at this time of year ...
See ya!